FOSSILS UNCOVERED!

DINOSAUR EATER

SUPERCROC DISCOVERY

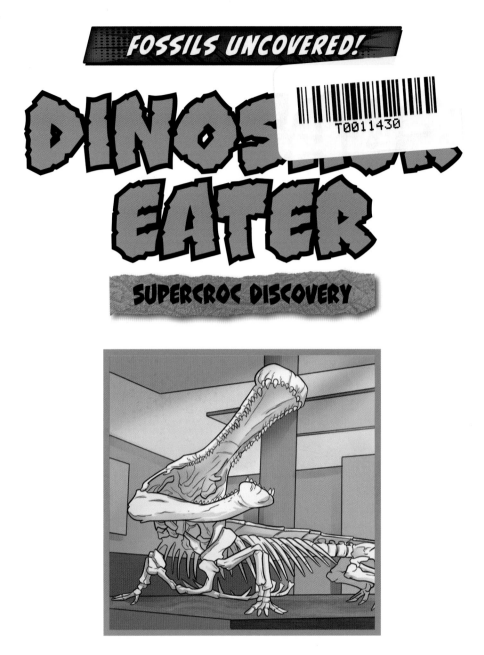

By Sarah Eason
Illustrated by Diego Vaisberg

BEARPORT
PUBLISHING

Minneapolis, Minnesota

Credits: 20b, © Warpaint/Shutterstock; 21t, © Herschel Hoffmeyer/Shutterstock; 21b, © Daniel Eskridge/Shutterstock; 22l, © Kriengsak Wiriyakrieng/Shutterstock; 22r, © Microgen/Shutterstock; 23b, © LegART/Shutterstock.

Editor: Jennifer Sanderson
Proofreader: Harriet McGregor
Designer: Paul Myerscough
Picture Researcher: Rachel Blount

DISCLAIMER: This graphic story is a dramatization based on true events. It is intended to give the reader a sense of the narrative rather than a presentation of actual details as they occurred.

Library of Congress Cataloging-in-Publication Data

Names: Eason, Sarah, author. | Vaisberg, Diego, 1981- illustrator.
Title: Dinosaur eater : supercroc discovery / by Sarah Eason ; illustrated
  by Diego Vaisberg.
Description: Bear claw books. | Minneapolis, Minnesota : Bearport
  Publishing Company, [2022] | Series: Fossils uncovered! | Includes
  bibliographical references and index.
Identifiers: LCCN 2021030929 (print) | LCCN 2021030930 (ebook) | ISBN
  9781636913339 (library binding) | ISBN 9781636913407 (paperback) | ISBN
  9781636913476 (ebook)
Subjects: LCSH: Sarcosuchus imperator--Juvenile literature.
Classification: LCC QE862.C8 E27 2022 (print) | LCC QE862.C8 (ebook) |
  DDC 567.9/8--dc23
LC record available at https://lccn.loc.gov/2021030929
LC ebook record available at https://lccn.loc.gov/2021030930

For more information, write to Bearport Publishing, 5357 Penn Avenue South, Minneapolis, MN 55419. Printed in the United States of America.

CONTENTS

CHAPTER 1

A SKULL IN THE SAND

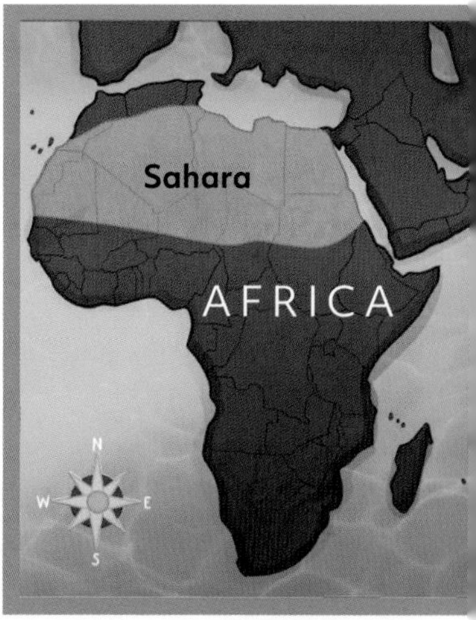
Sahara
AFRICA
N
W
E
S

In 1995, **paleontologist** Paul Sereno and his team were searching for dinosaur bones in the desert sands of the Sahara.

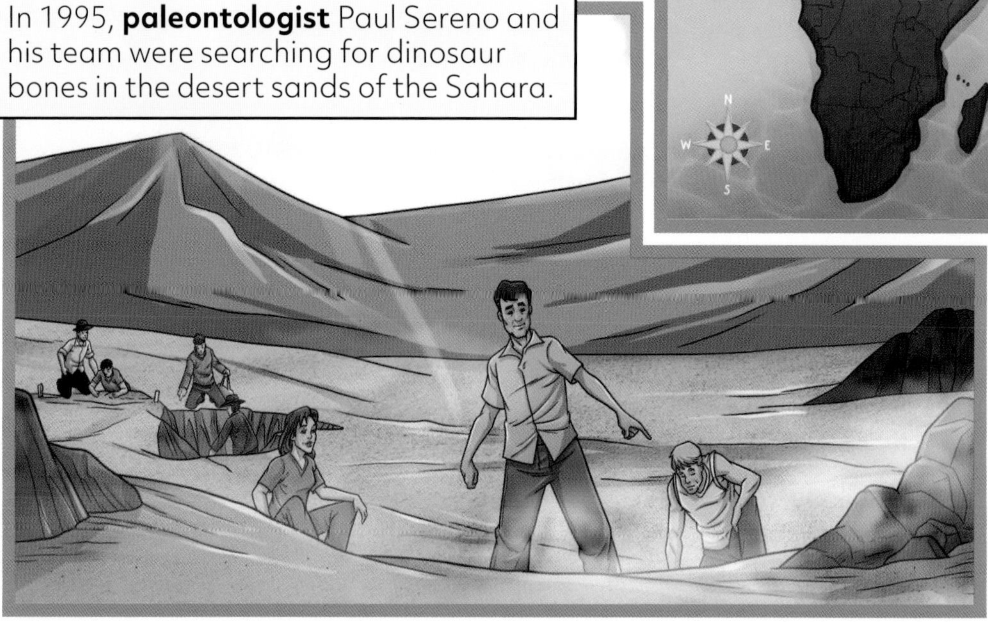

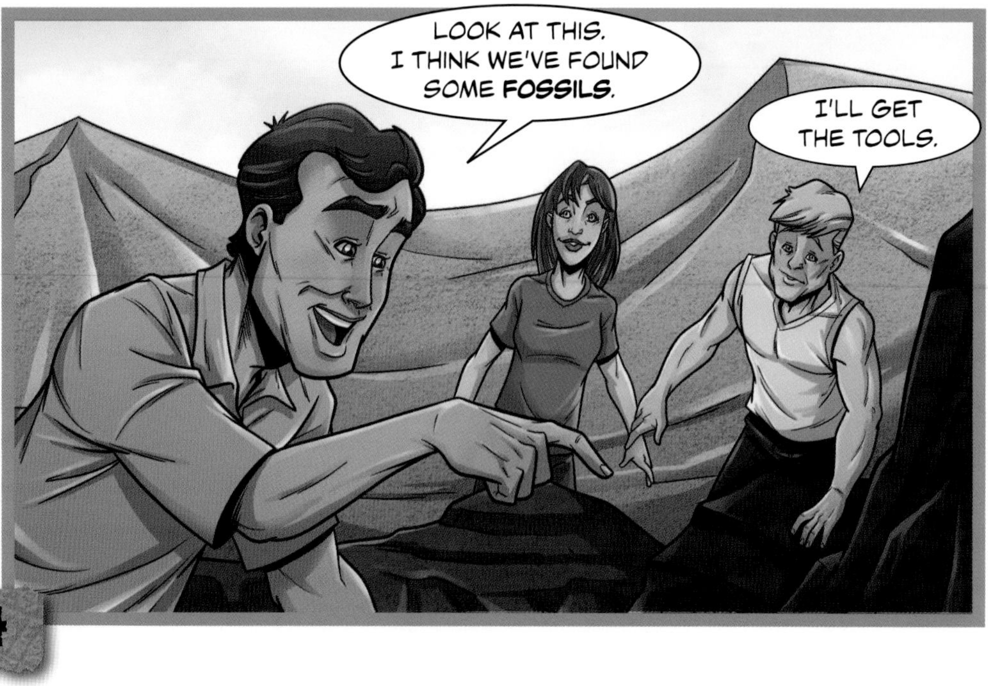
LOOK AT THIS. I THINK WE'VE FOUND SOME **FOSSILS**.
I'LL GET THE TOOLS.

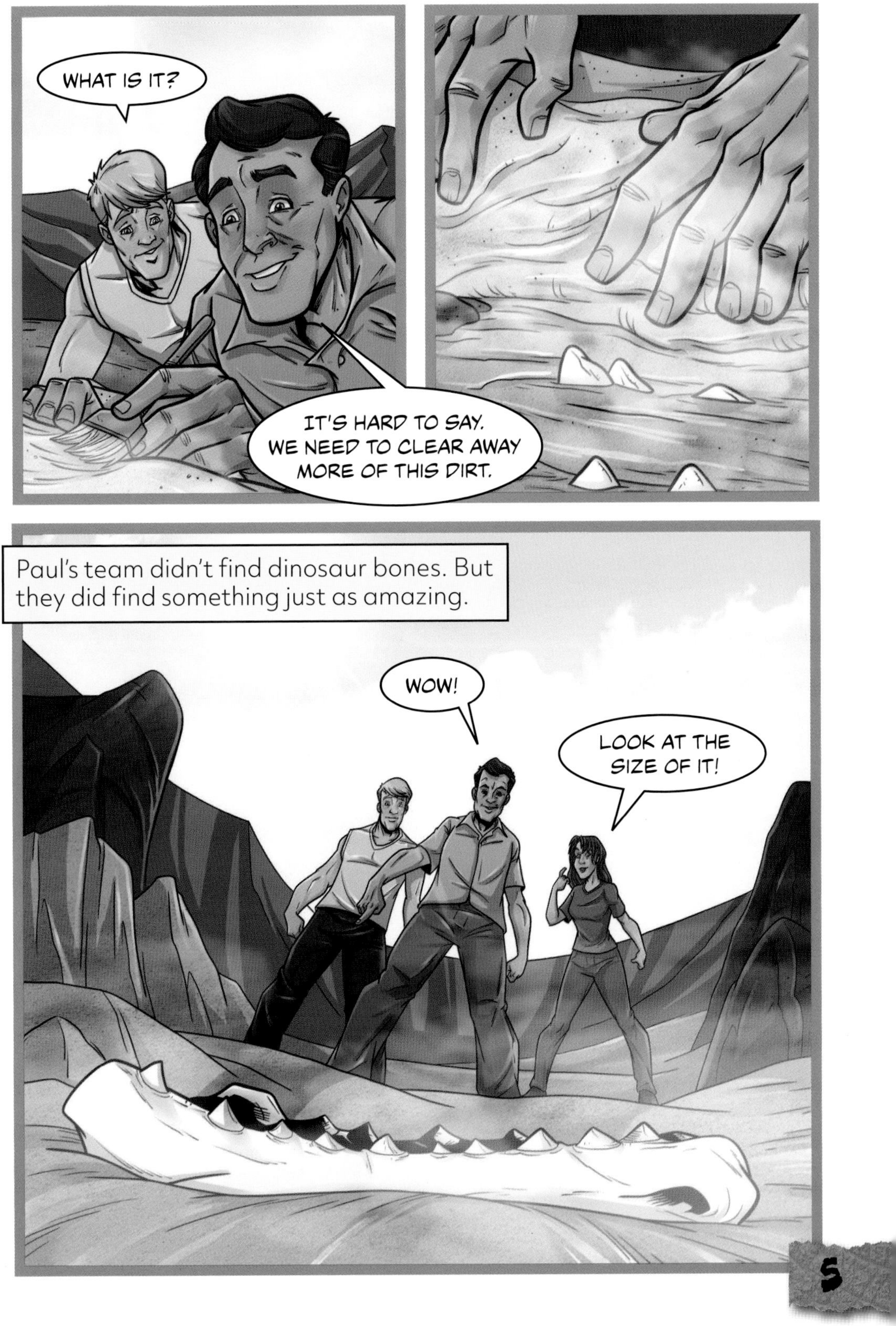
WHAT IS IT?
IT'S HARD TO SAY. WE NEED TO CLEAR AWAY MORE OF THIS DIRT.
Paul's team didn't find dinosaur bones. But they did find something just as amazing.
WOW!
LOOK AT THE SIZE OF IT!

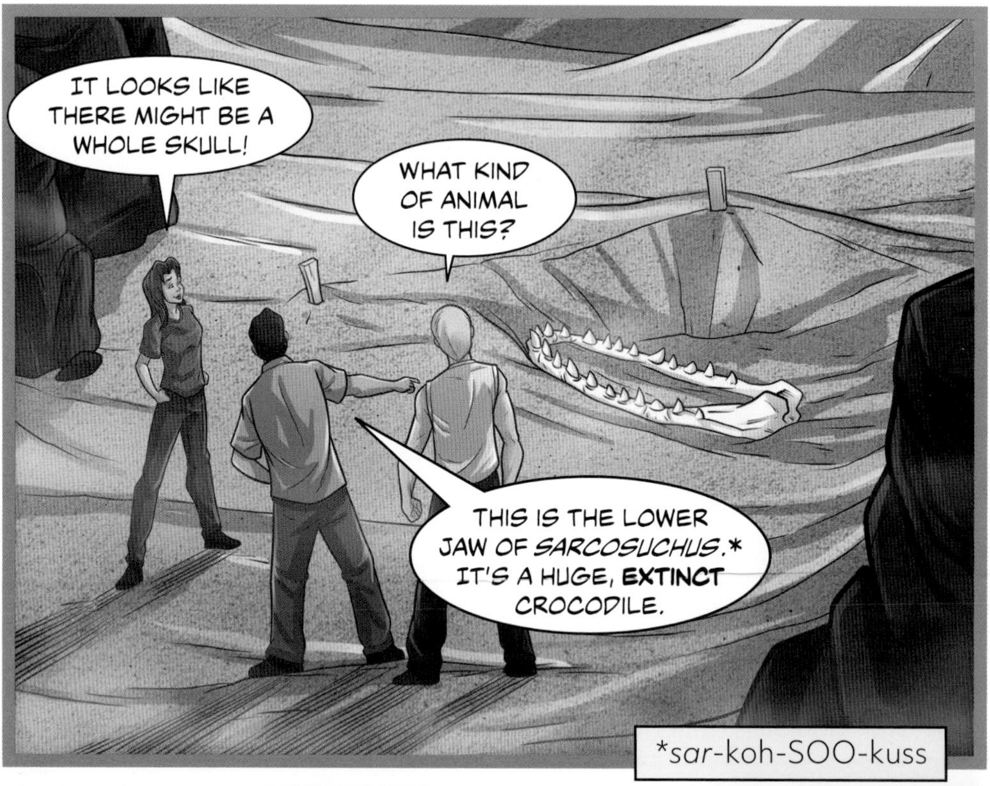
IT LOOKS LIKE THERE MIGHT BE A WHOLE SKULL!
WHAT KIND OF ANIMAL IS THIS?
THIS IS THE LOWER JAW OF *SARCOSUCHUS*.* IT'S A HUGE, **EXTINCT** CROCODILE.
*sar-koh-SOO-kuss

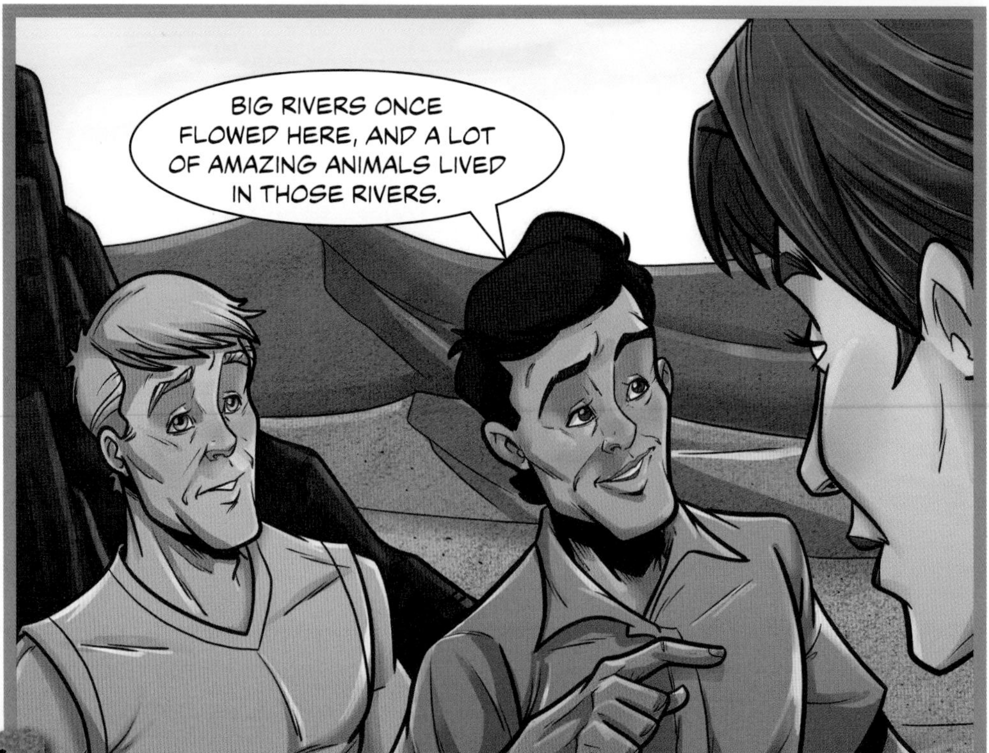
BIG RIVERS ONCE FLOWED HERE, AND A LOT OF AMAZING ANIMALS LIVED IN THOSE RIVERS.

Paul stretched out in the sand next to the enormous jawbone.

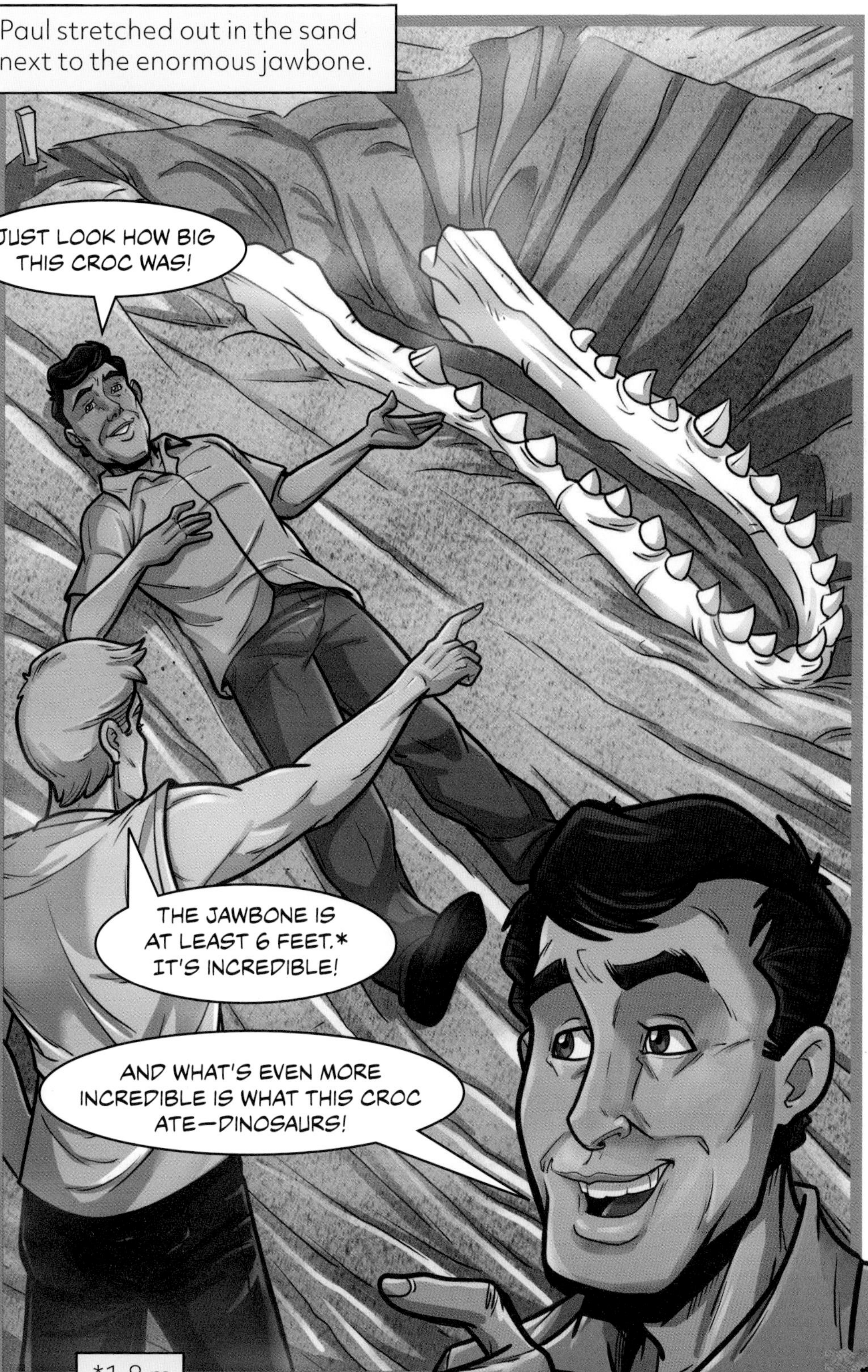
JUST LOOK HOW BIG THIS CROC WAS!
THE JAWBONE IS AT LEAST 6 FEET.* IT'S INCREDIBLE!
AND WHAT'S EVEN MORE INCREDIBLE IS WHAT THIS CROC ATE—DINOSAURS!

*1.8 m

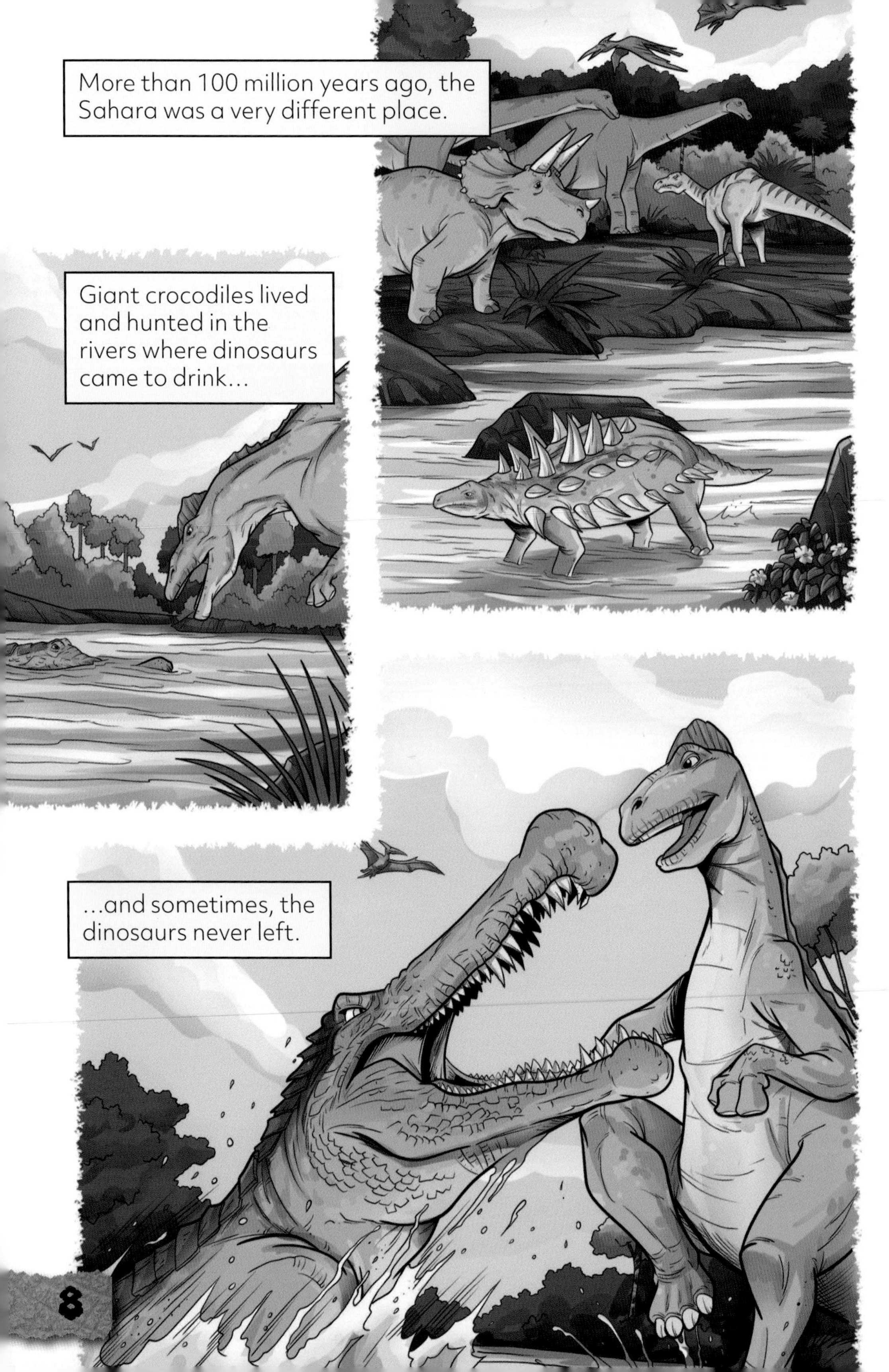
More than 100 million years ago, the Sahara was a very different place.
Giant crocodiles lived and hunted in the rivers where dinosaurs came to drink…
…and sometimes, the dinosaurs never left.

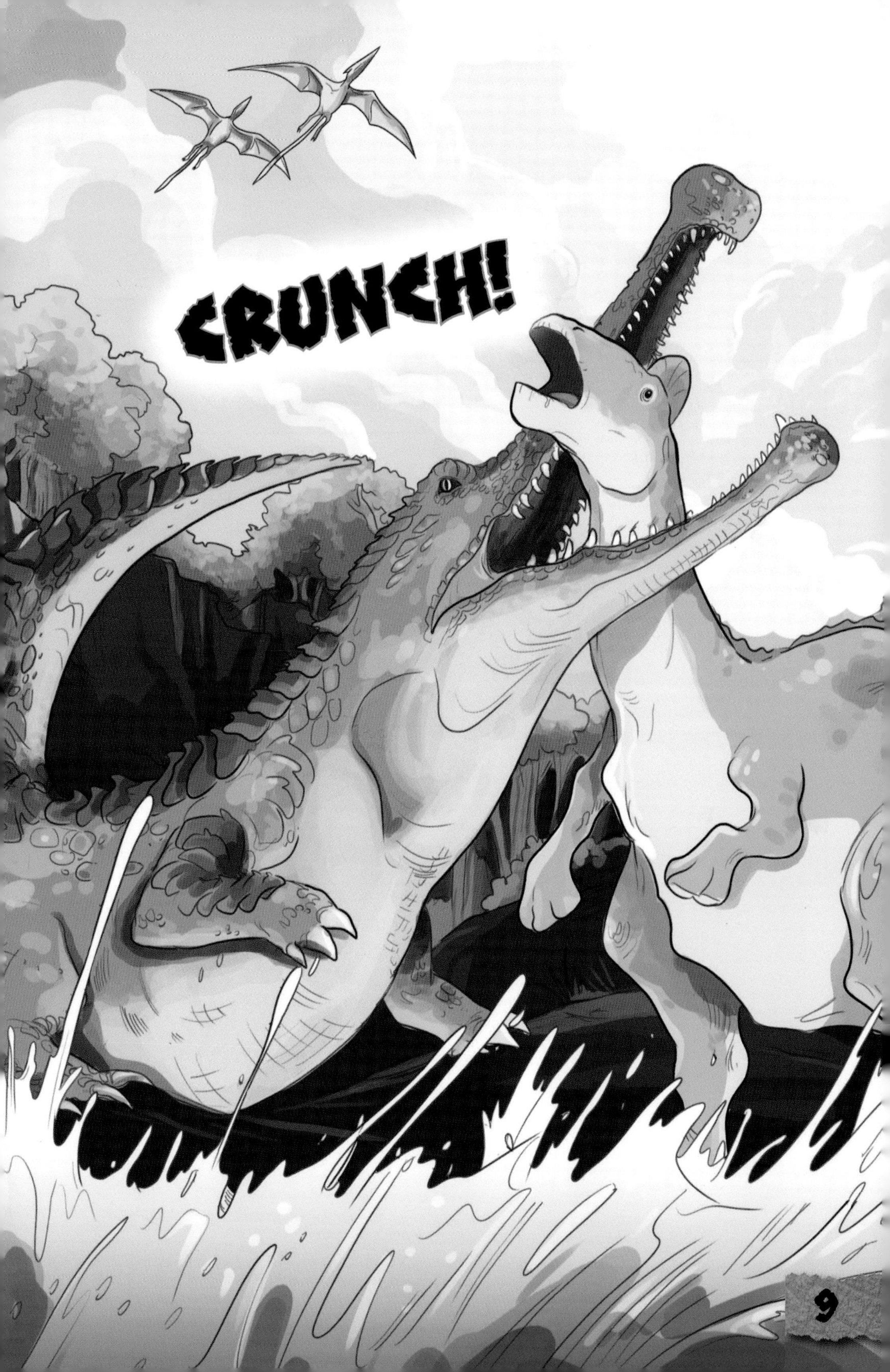
CRUNCH!

CHAPTER 2

UNDERSTANDING SUPERCROC

Paul wanted to learn more about the **ancient** crocodile nicknamed SuperCroc. During trips back to the Sahara in 1997 and 2000, he and his team dug up many more fossils.

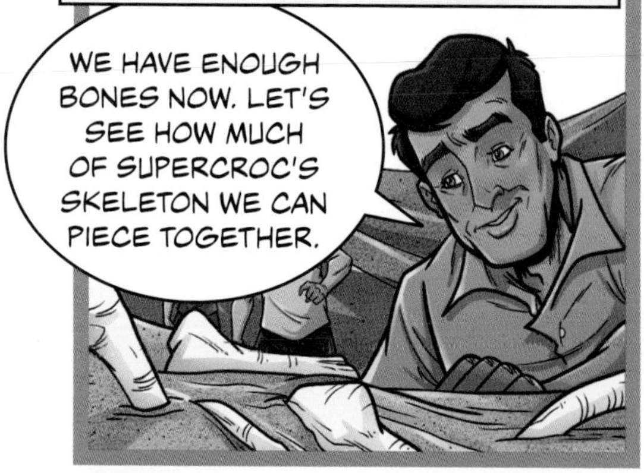
WE HAVE ENOUGH BONES NOW. LET'S SEE HOW MUCH OF SUPERCROC'S SKELETON WE CAN PIECE TOGETHER.

The team sent the fossils to the University of Chicago, where Paul and others could study them.

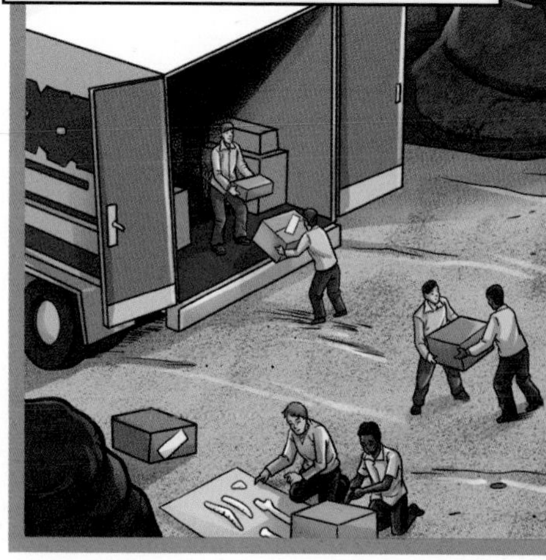

Slowly, Paul and his team learned where each bone belonged in the fossilized skeleton and which bones were missing.

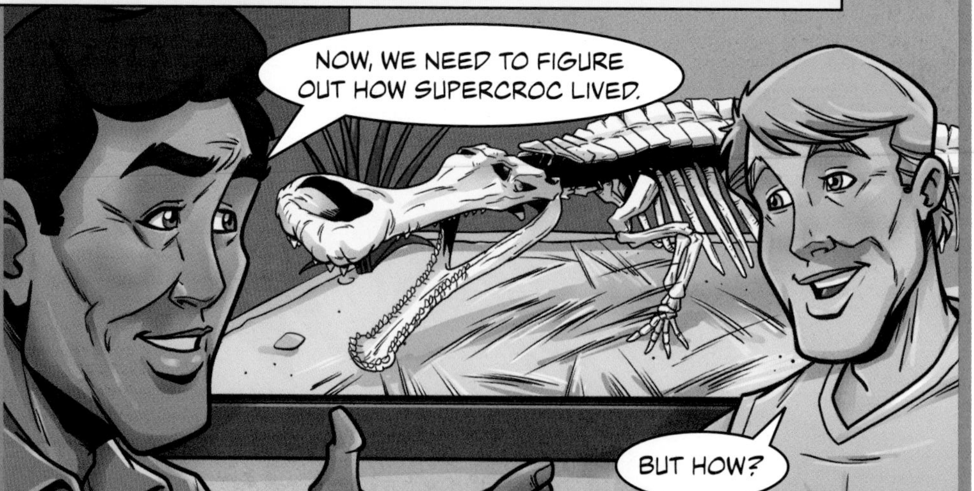
NOW, WE NEED TO FIGURE OUT HOW SUPERCROC LIVED.
BUT HOW?

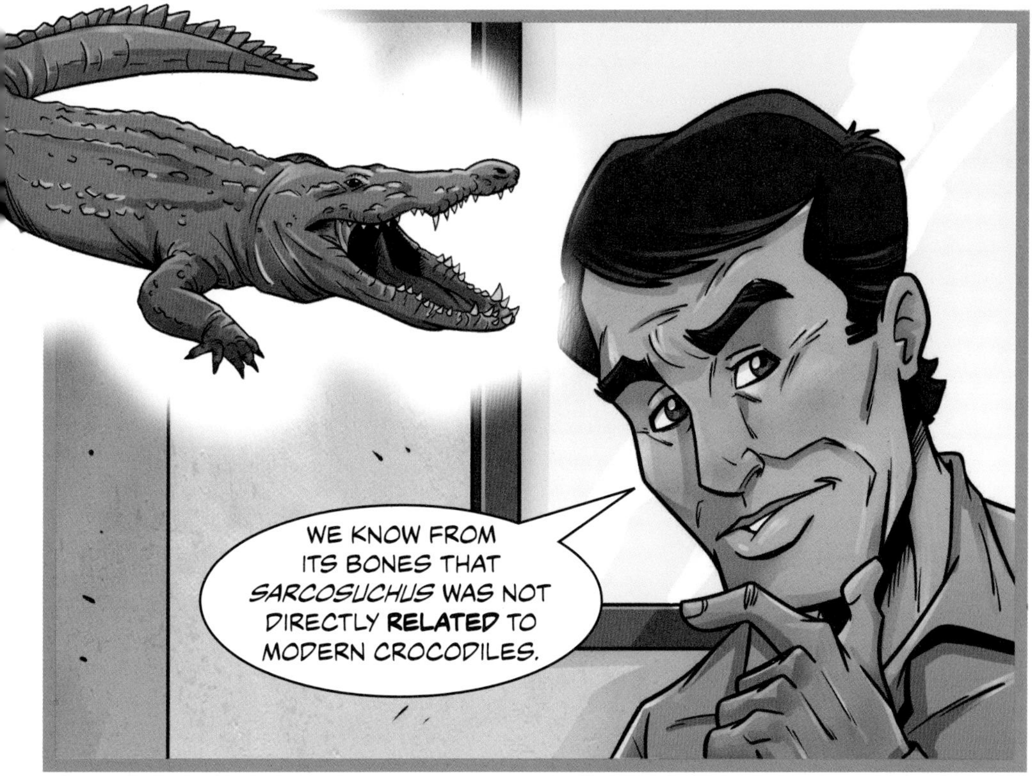
WE KNOW FROM ITS BONES THAT *SARCOSUCHUS* WAS NOT DIRECTLY **RELATED** TO MODERN CROCODILES.

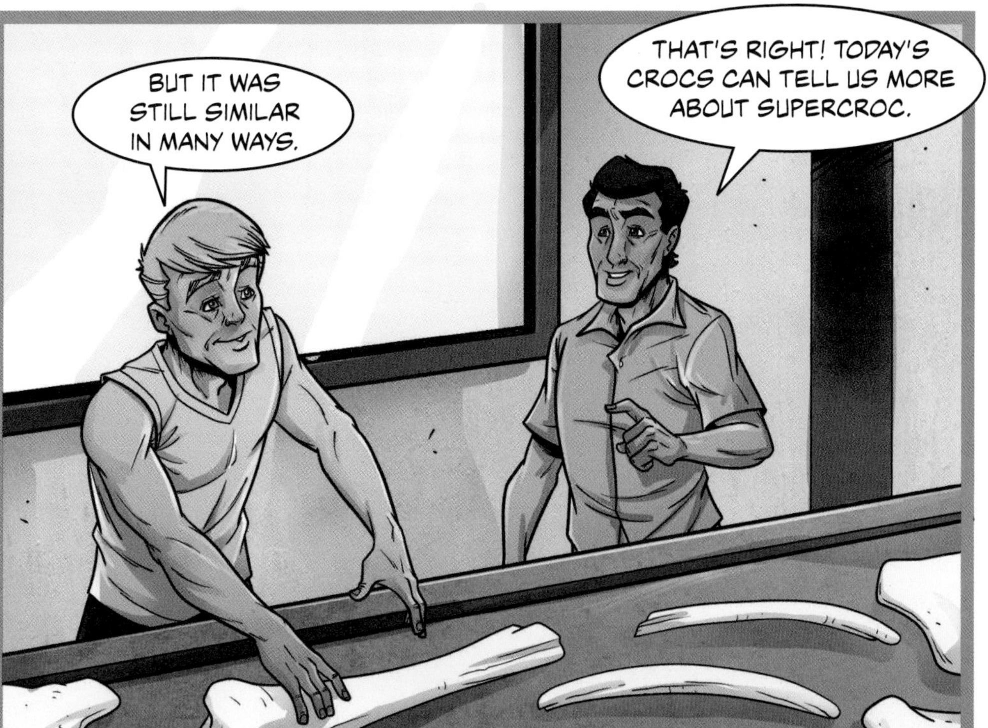
BUT IT WAS STILL SIMILAR IN MANY WAYS.
THAT'S RIGHT! TODAY'S CROCS CAN TELL US MORE ABOUT SUPERCROC.

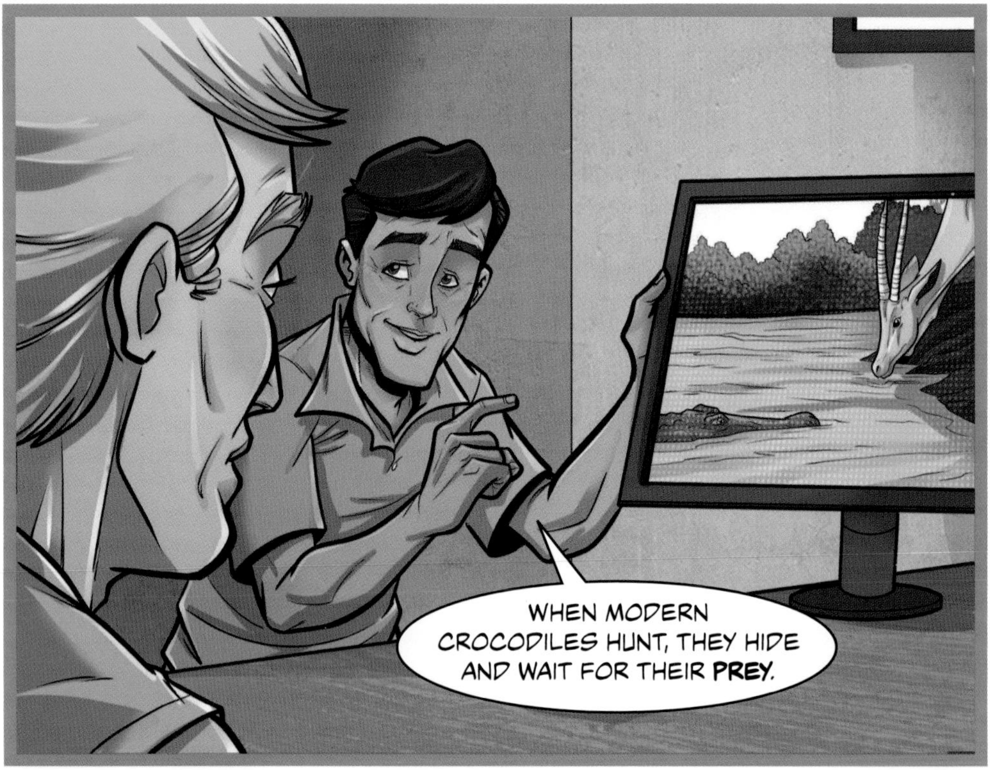
WHEN MODERN CROCODILES HUNT, THEY HIDE AND WAIT FOR THEIR **PREY**.

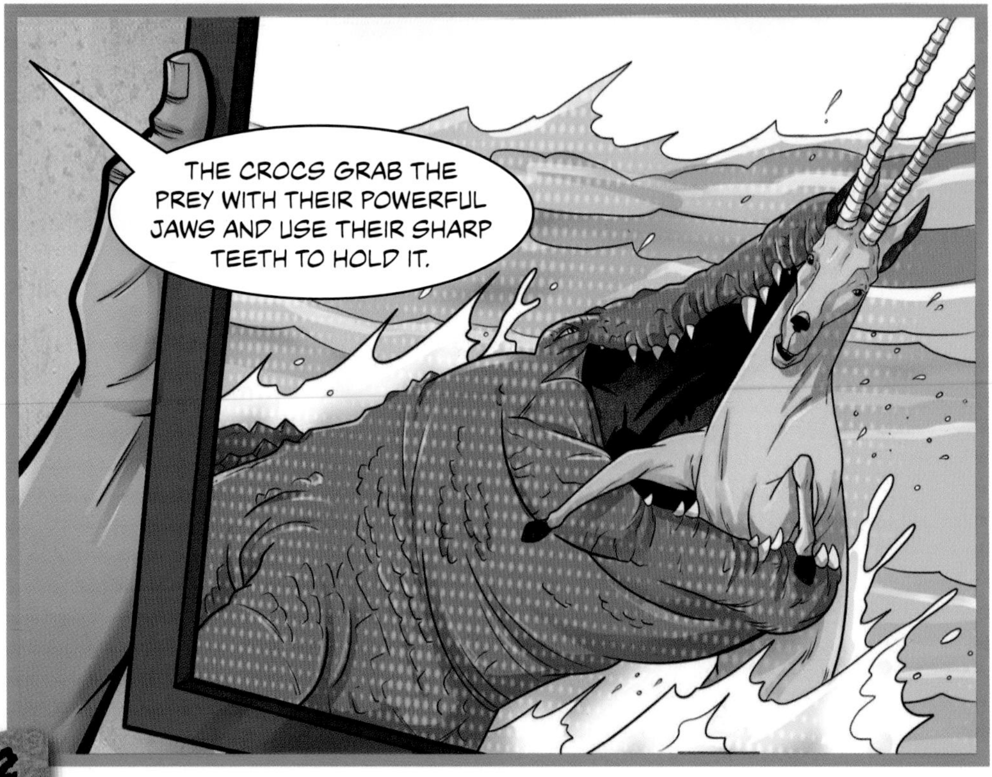
THE CROCS GRAB THE PREY WITH THEIR POWERFUL JAWS AND USE THEIR SHARP TEETH TO HOLD IT.

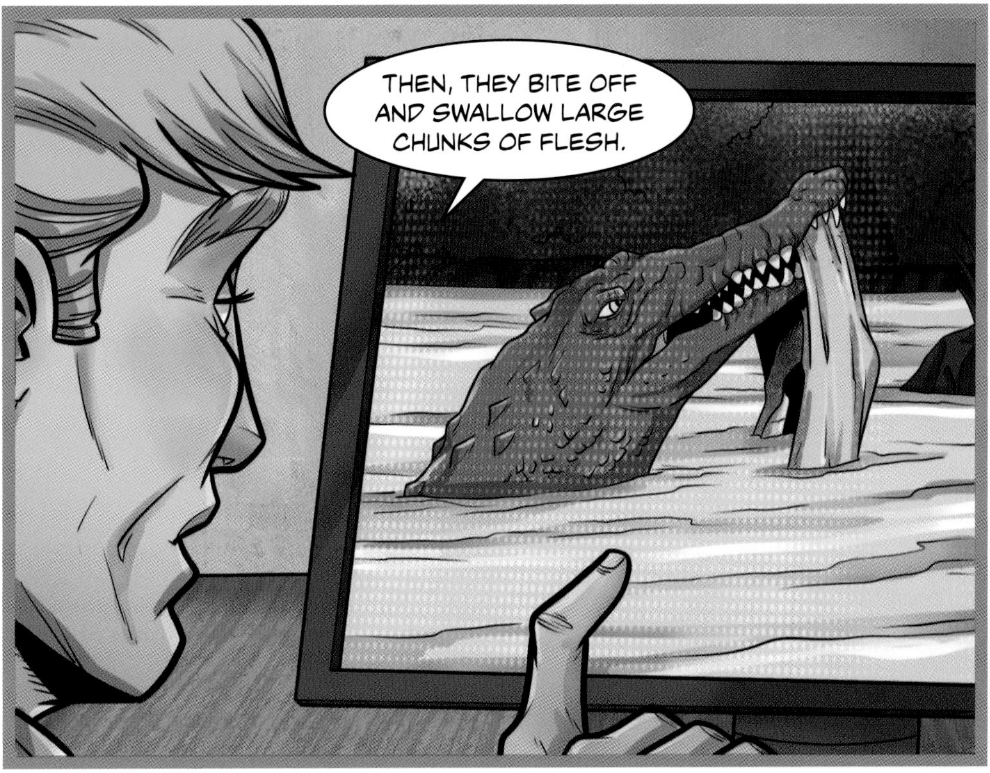
THEN, THEY BITE OFF AND SWALLOW LARGE CHUNKS OF FLESH.

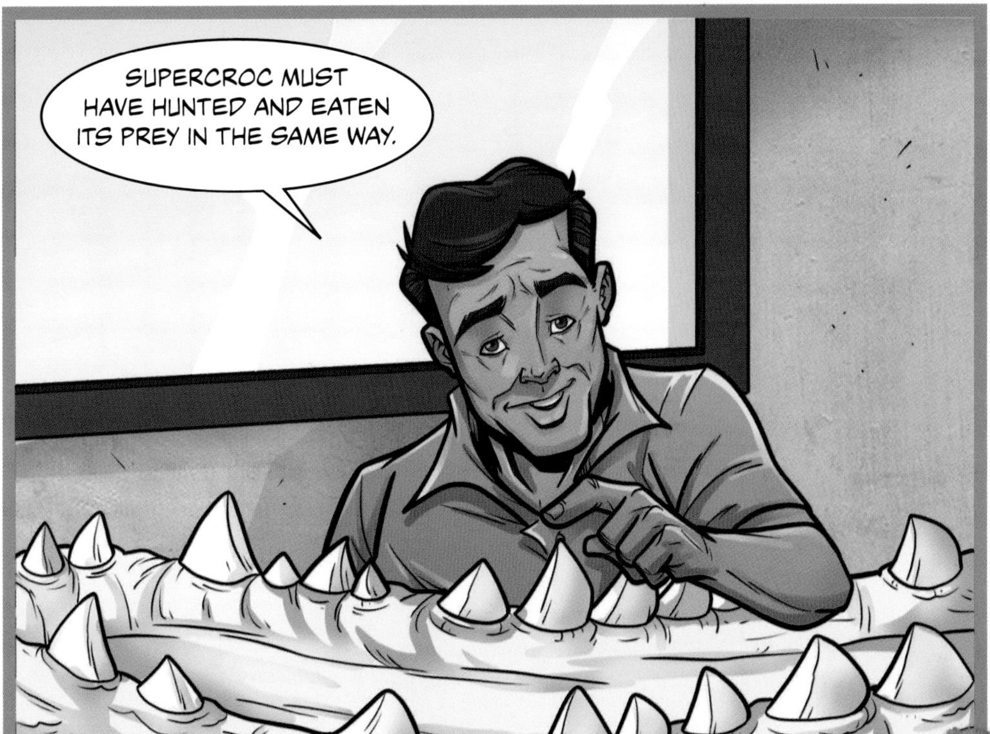
SUPERCROC MUST HAVE HUNTED AND EATEN ITS PREY IN THE SAME WAY.

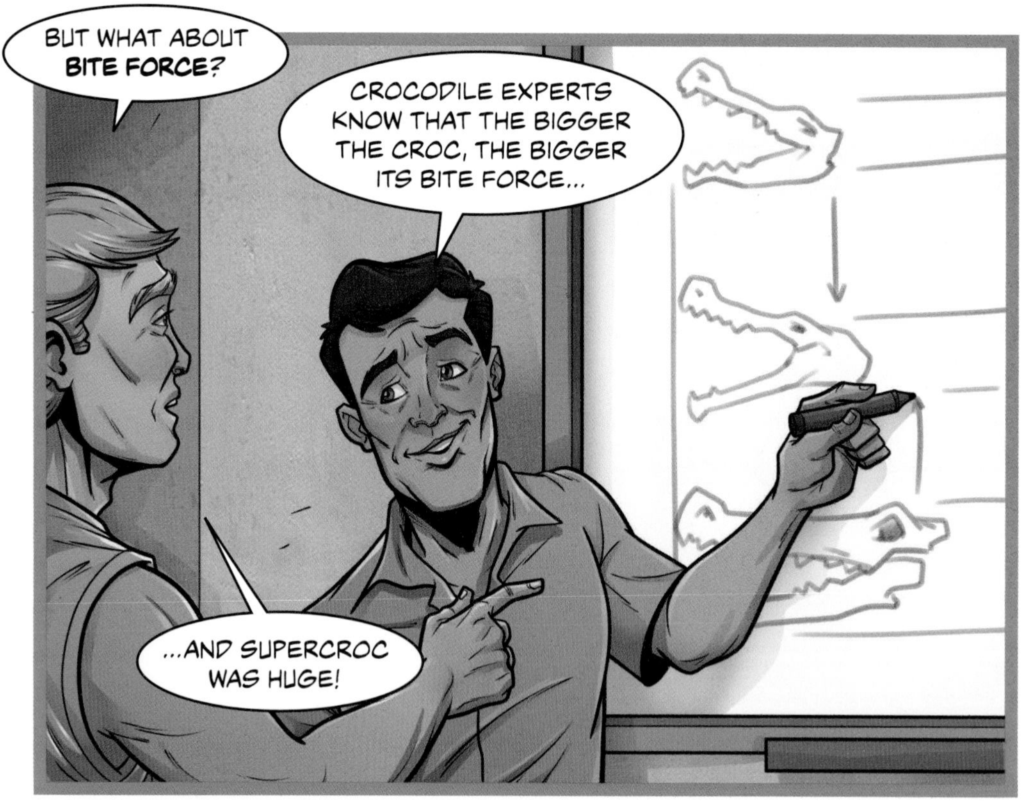
BUT WHAT ABOUT **BITE FORCE**?
CROCODILE EXPERTS KNOW THAT THE BIGGER THE CROC, THE BIGGER ITS BITE FORCE...
...AND SUPERCROC WAS HUGE!

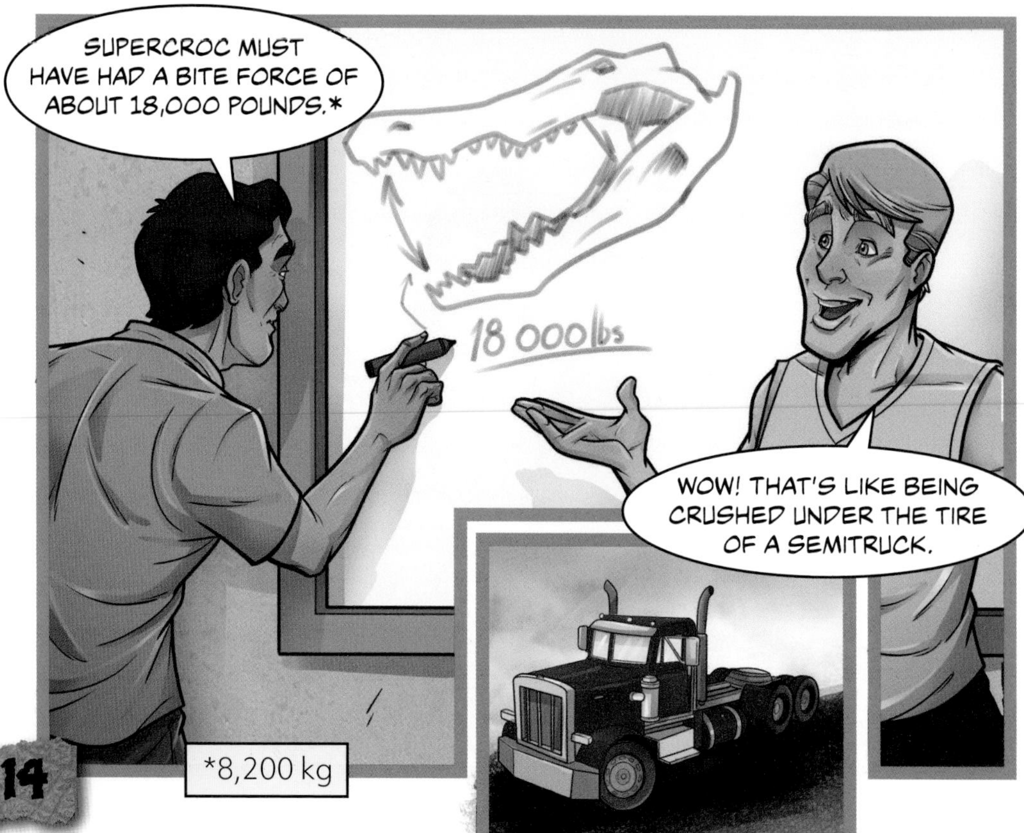
SUPERCROC MUST HAVE HAD A BITE FORCE OF ABOUT 18,000 POUNDS.*
18 000lbs
WOW! THAT'S LIKE BEING CRUSHED UNDER THE TIRE OF A SEMITRUCK.

*8,200 kg

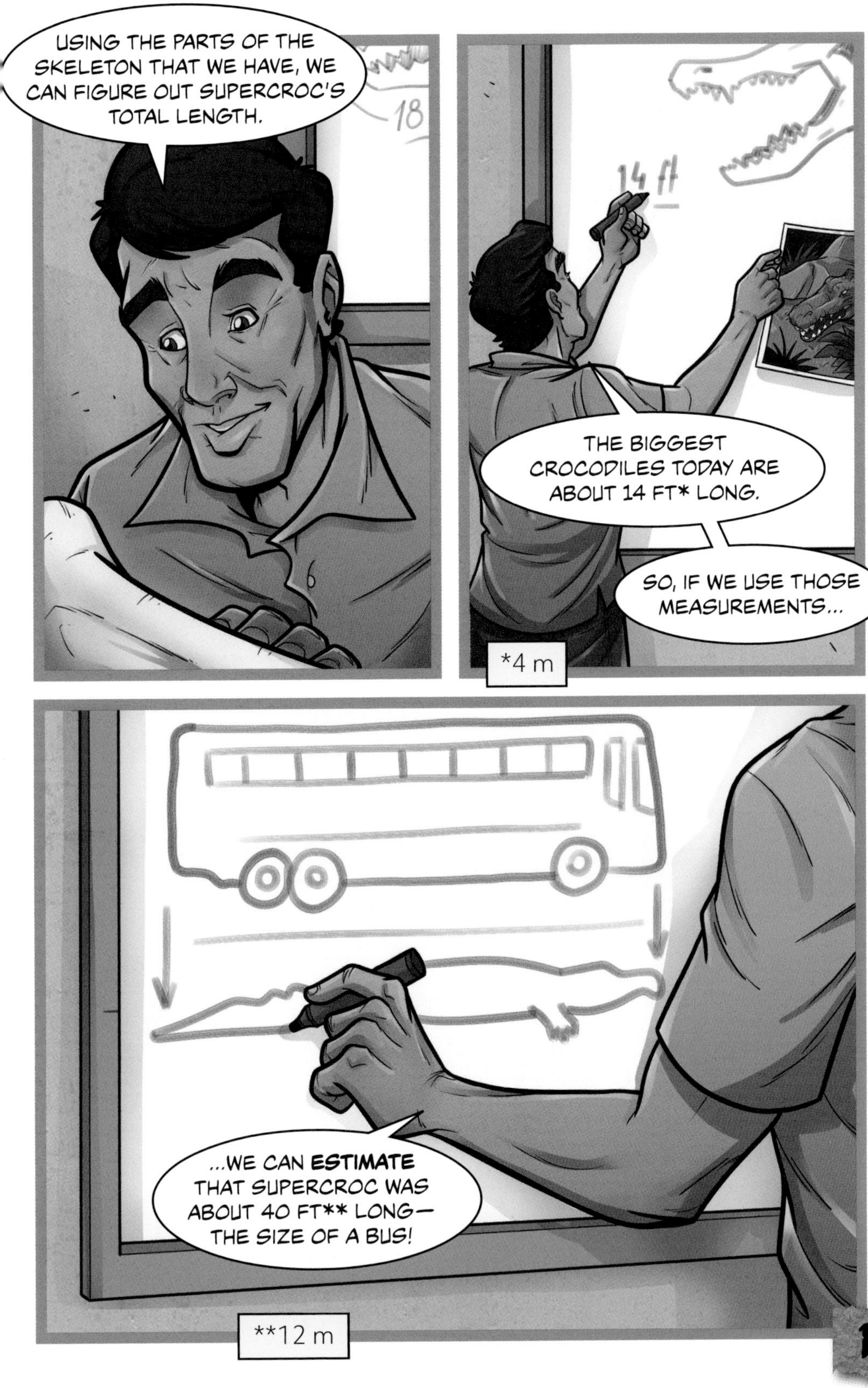
USING THE PARTS OF THE SKELETON THAT WE HAVE, WE CAN FIGURE OUT SUPERCROC'S TOTAL LENGTH.
14 ft
THE BIGGEST CROCODILES TODAY ARE ABOUT 14 FT* LONG.
SO, IF WE USE THOSE MEASUREMENTS...
*4 m
...WE CAN **ESTIMATE** THAT SUPERCROC WAS ABOUT 40 FT** LONG—THE SIZE OF A BUS!
**12 m

CHAPTER 3

BACK TO LIFE!

Soon, Paul came up with an exciting plan.

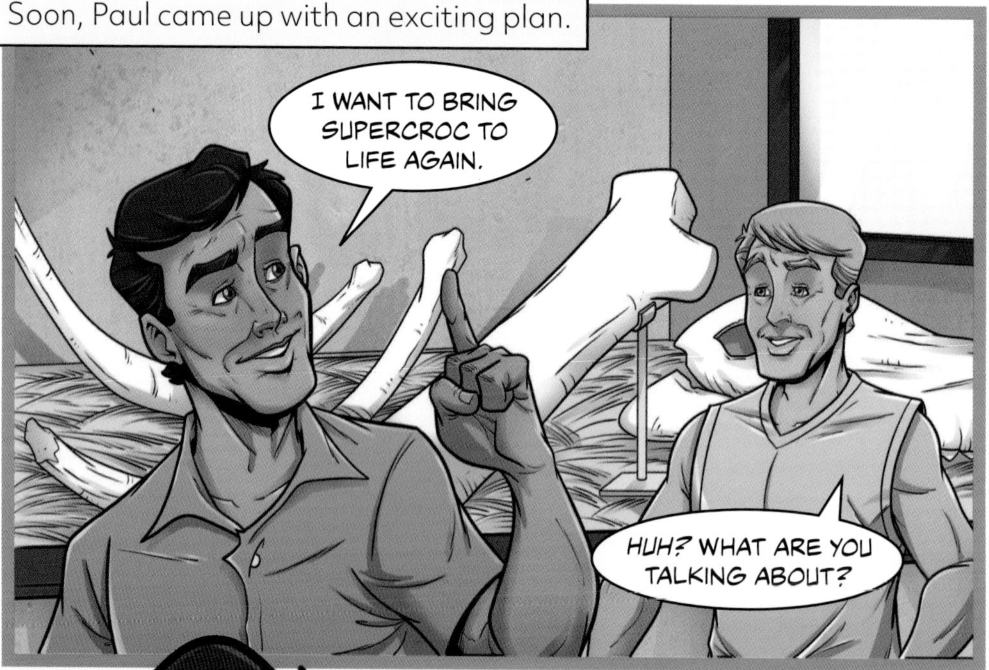
I WANT TO BRING SUPERCROC TO LIFE AGAIN.
HUH? WHAT ARE YOU TALKING ABOUT?

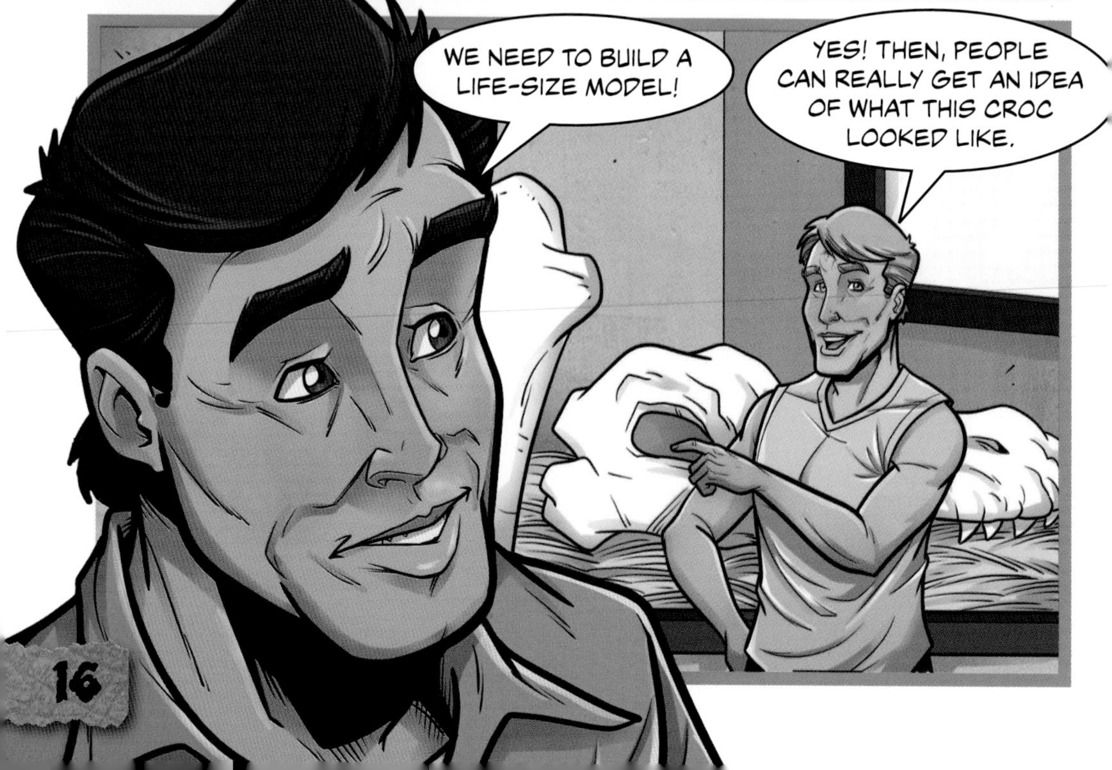
WE NEED TO BUILD A LIFE-SIZE MODEL!
YES! THEN, PEOPLE CAN REALLY GET AN IDEA OF WHAT THIS CROC LOOKED LIKE.

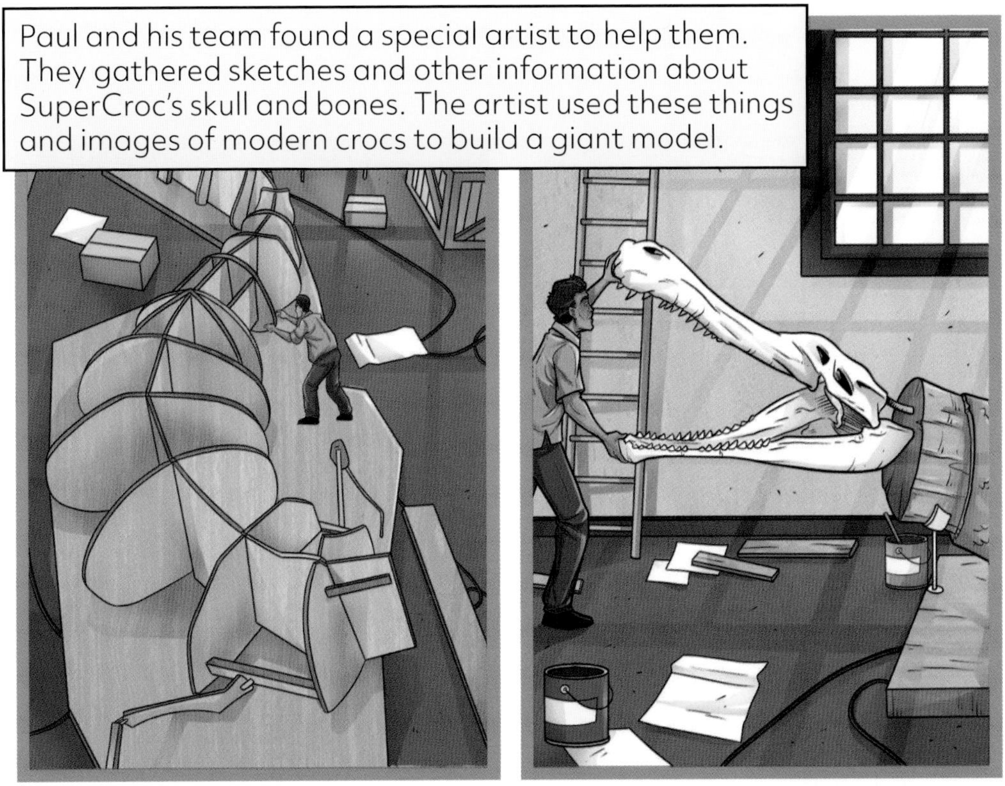
Paul and his team found a special artist to help them. They gathered sketches and other information about SuperCroc's skull and bones. The artist used these things and images of modern crocs to build a giant model.

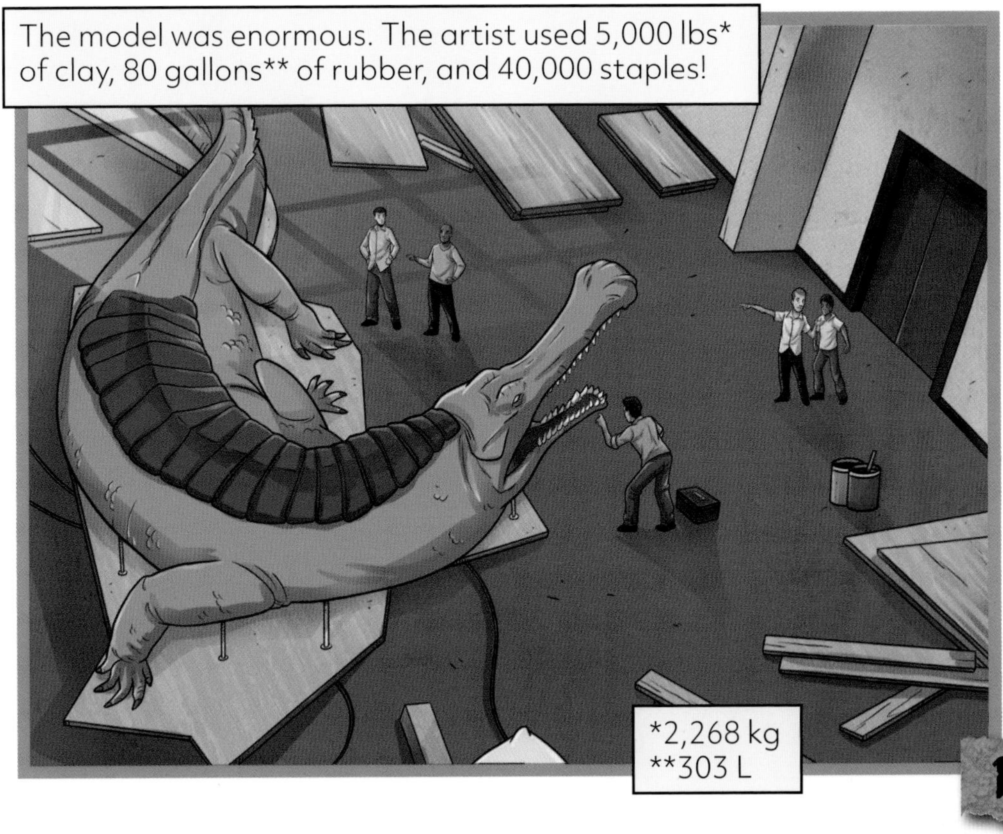
The model was enormous. The artist used 5,000 lbs* of clay, 80 gallons** of rubber, and 40,000 staples!
*2,268 kg
**303 L

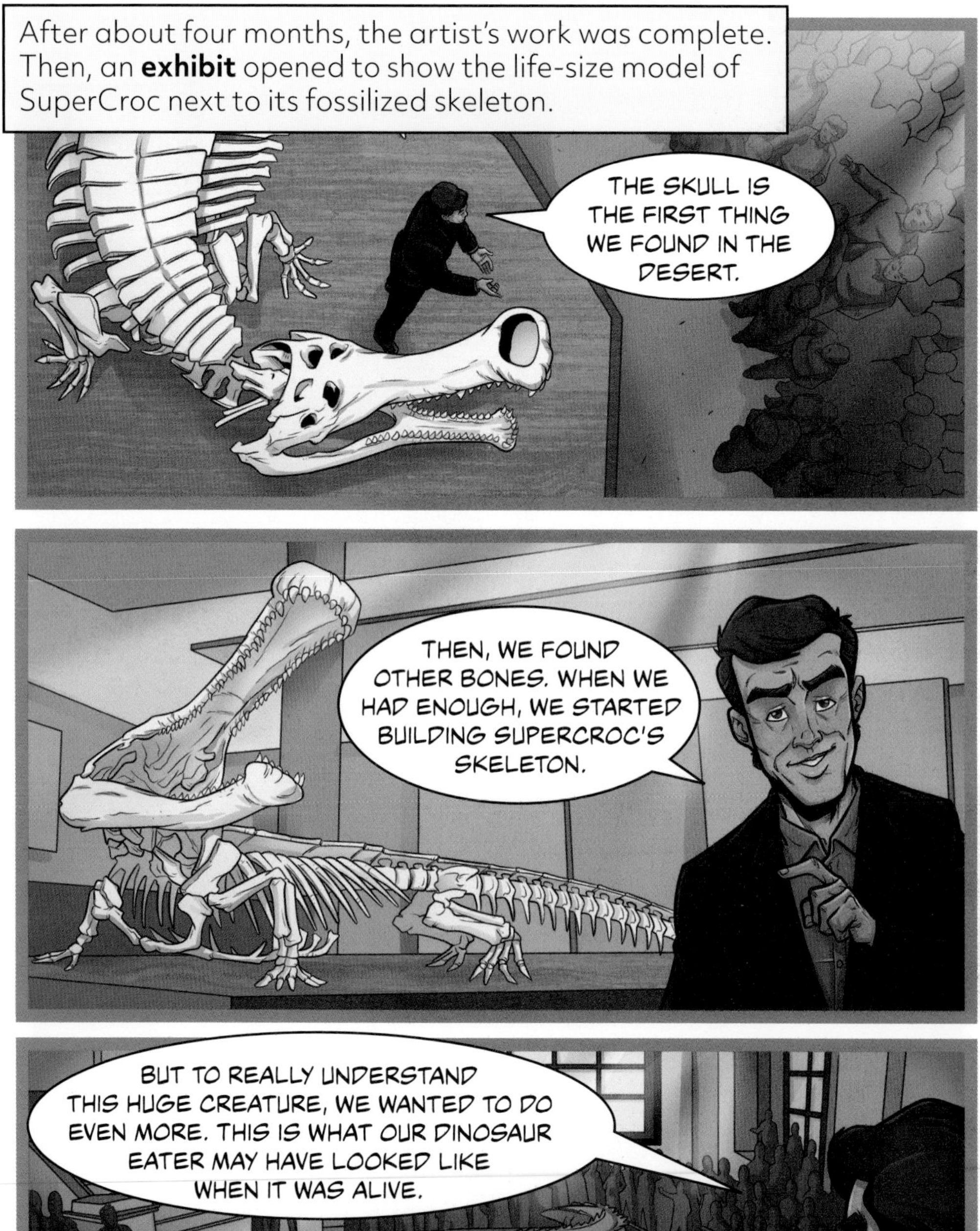

After about four months, the artist's work was complete. Then, an **exhibit** opened to show the life-size model of SuperCroc next to its fossilized skeleton.
THE SKULL IS THE FIRST THING WE FOUND IN THE DESERT.
THEN, WE FOUND OTHER BONES. WHEN WE HAD ENOUGH, WE STARTED BUILDING SUPERCROC'S SKELETON.
BUT TO REALLY UNDERSTAND THIS HUGE CREATURE, WE WANTED TO DO EVEN MORE. THIS IS WHAT OUR DINOSAUR EATER MAY HAVE LOOKED LIKE WHEN IT WAS ALIVE.

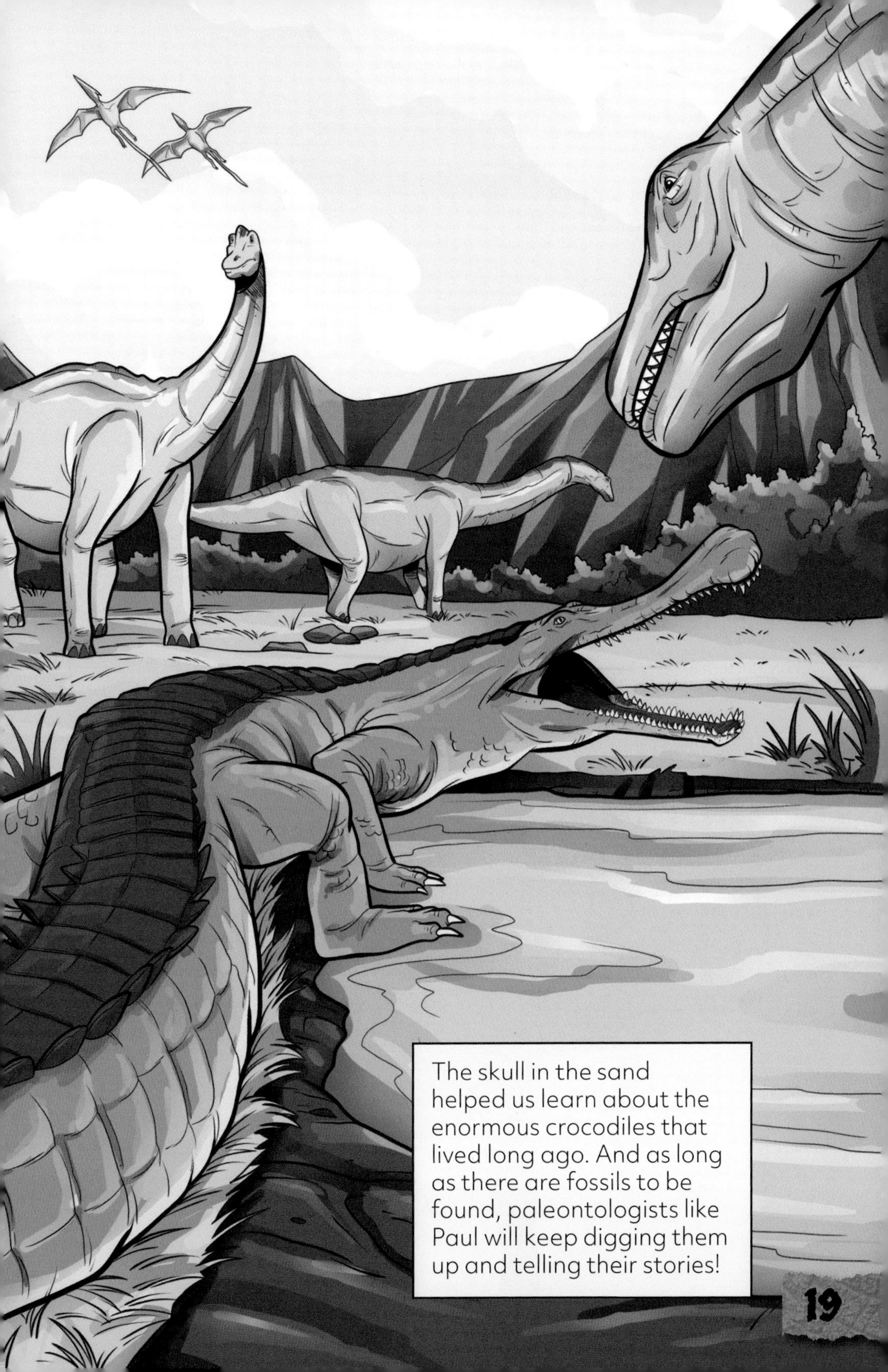
The skull in the sand helped us learn about the enormous crocodiles that lived long ago. And as long as there are fossils to be found, paleontologists like Paul will keep digging them up and telling their stories!

Who Lived with SuperCroc?

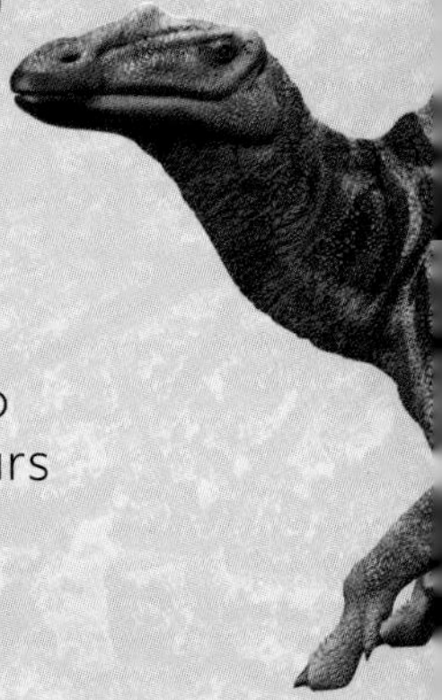

Dinosaurs lived on Earth for about 150 million years. Scientists divide the time in which the dinosaurs lived into three periods—the Triassic period (252 to 201 million years ago), the Jurassic period (201 to 145 million years ago), and the Cretaceous period (145 to 66 million years ago).

SuperCroc lived alongside dinosaurs during the early Cretaceous period. Here are three dinosaurs that shared SuperCroc's world.

NIGERSAURUS (*n*ee-zhair-SOR-uhss)

Drinking water along the riverbanks, this dinosaur would have had to keep an eye out for SuperCroc. What else do we know about *Nigersaurus*?

- This plant eater had a long neck.
- It had as many as 500 small teeth in its jaws.
- *Nigersaurus* walked on four legs.
- It was 30 ft (9 m) long.

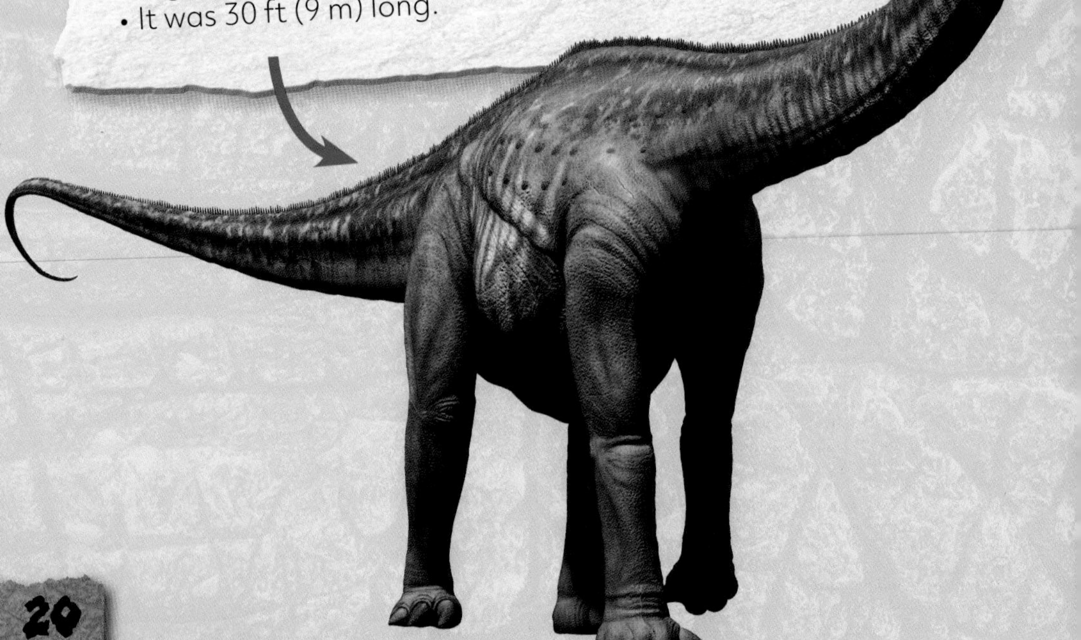

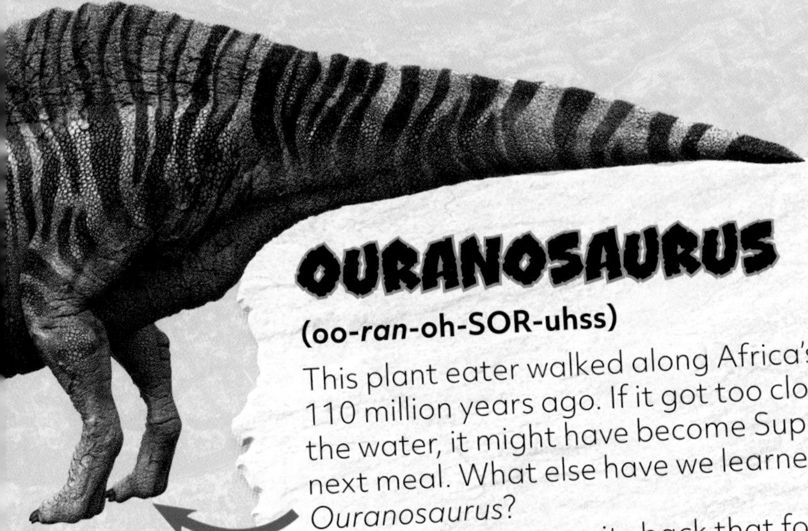

OURANOSAURUS

(oo-*ran*-oh-SOR-uhss)

This plant eater walked along Africa's riverbanks 110 million years ago. If it got too close to the water, it might have become SuperCroc's next meal. What else have we learned about *Ouranosaurus*?

- It had tall spines on its back that formed a sail.
- The sail may have been brightly colored.
- *Ouranosaurus* could move on two legs or four.
- It was 23 ft (7 m) long.

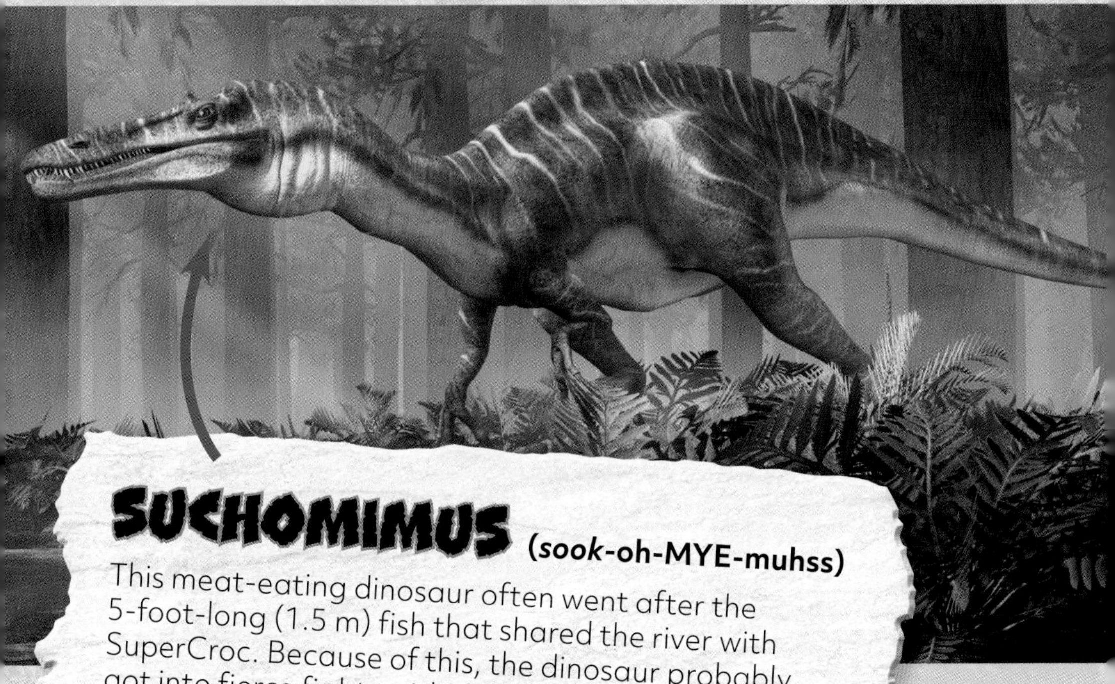

SUCHOMIMUS

(*sook*-oh-MYE-muhss)

This meat-eating dinosaur often went after the 5-foot-long (1.5 m) fish that shared the river with SuperCroc. Because of this, the dinosaur probably got into fierce fights with the giant crocodile. What are some other facts about *Suchomimus*?

- It had crocodile-like jaws and 1-foot-long (0.3 m) claws that helped it catch fish.
- Like *Ouranosaurus*, it had a sail along its back.
- It was 36 ft (11 m) long.

What Is Paleontology?

Paleontology is the study of fossils, which are what is left of things that lived millions of years ago. Fossils are found in rock. Paleontologists use special tools to carefully remove the fossils from the rock so they can study them. By studying fossils, paleontologists can figure out where a plant or animal lived, what it looked like, and how it lived.

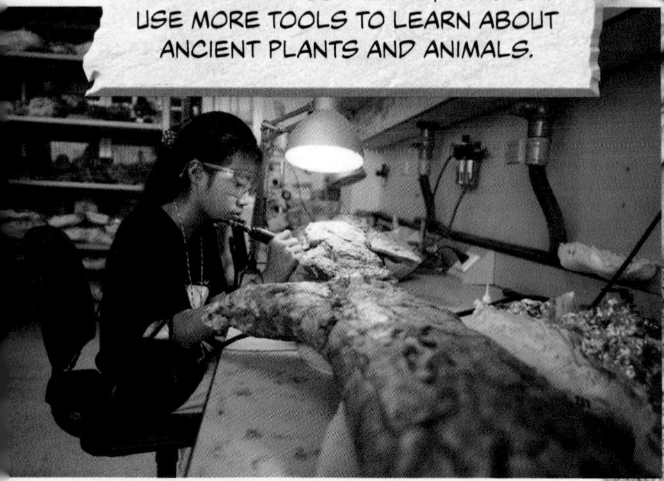

SOMETIMES PALEONTOLOGISTS STUDY FOSSILS IN LABS. THERE, THEY CAN USE MORE TOOLS TO LEARN ABOUT ANCIENT PLANTS AND ANIMALS.

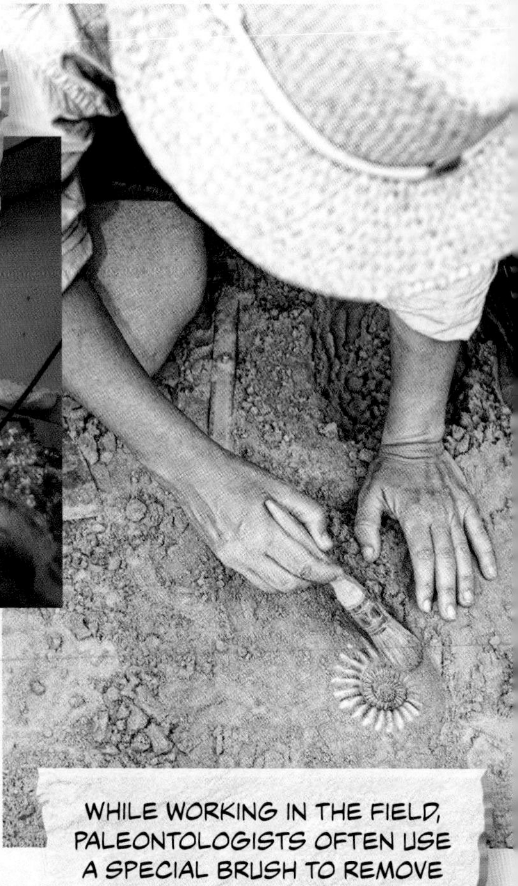

WHILE WORKING IN THE FIELD, PALEONTOLOGISTS OFTEN USE A SPECIAL BRUSH TO REMOVE LOOSE PIECES OF ROCK AND DUST FROM FOSSILS.

Fossils can show how living things changed over time, too. Paleontologists can use fossils to find out what happened to an **environment** in the past and how living things **adapted** to the changes.

Glossary

adapted changed in order to handle new conditions

ancient from a very long time ago

bite force the power of an animal's bite

environment the conditions that surround a living thing

estimate to make a careful guess about the size, cost, or value of something

exhibit something that is shown to many people

extinct when a type of plant or animal has died out and there are no more of them alive on Earth

fossils the hardened remains of things that lived long ago

paleontologist a scientist who studies fossils to find out about life in the past

prey animals that are hunted and eaten by other animals

related belonging to the same family

FOSSILS HELP SCIENTISTS UNDERSTAND WHAT DINOSAURS LOOKED LIKE. THEY CAN USE THIS INFORMATION TO BUILD MODELS OF THEM.

Index

Read More

Hudd, Emily. *How Long Does It Take to Make a Fossil? (How Long Does It Take?)*. North Mankato, MN: Capstone Press, 2020.

Leavitt, Amie Jane. *Dream Jobs If You Like Dinosaurs (Dream Jobs for Future You)*. North Mankato, MN: Capstone Press, 2021.

Suen, Anastasia. *Mega Creatures of Ancient Lands (Mega-Cool Megafauna)*. Vero Beach, FL: Rourke Educational Media, 2020.

Learn More Online

1. Go to **www.factsurfer.com** or scan the QR code below.
2. Enter "**Dinosaur Eater**" into the search box.
3. Click on the cover of this book to see a list of websites.